Najc

D1253480

It's My STATE!

NEW JERSEY

The Garden State

Derek Miller, David C. King,
William McGeveran, and Greg Clinton

Cavendish
Square

New York

Published in 2020 by Cavendish Square Publishing, LLC
243 5th Avenue, Suite 136, New York, NY 10016

Library of Congress Cataloging-in-Publication Data

Names: Miller, Derek, author.
Title: New Jersey / Derek Miller, David C. King, William McGeveran, and Greg Clinton.
Description: Fourth edition. | New York : Cavendish Square, [2020] |
Series: It's my state! | Includes bibliographical references and index. | Audience: Grades 3-5.
Identifiers: LCCN 2018039114 (print) | LCCN 2018039368 (ebook) |
ISBN 9781502642370 (ebook) | ISBN 9781502642363 (library bound) |
ISBN 9781502644497 (pbk.)
Subjects: LCSH: New Jersey--Juvenile literature.
Classification: LCC F134.3 (ebook) | LCC F134.3 .K56 2020 (print) | DDC 974.9--dc23
LC record available at https://lccn.loc.gov/2018039114

Editorial Director: David McNamara
Editor: Caitlyn Miller
Copy Editor: Nathan Heidelberger
Associate Art Director: Alan Sliwinski
Designer: Jessica Nevins
Production Coordinator: Karol Szymczuk
Photo Research: J8 Media

It's My STATE!

Table of Contents

SNAPSHOT
NEW JERSEY

The Garden State

Statehood

December 18, 1787

Population

9,005,644 (2017 census estimate)

Capital

Trenton

State Seal

Adopted in 1928, the Great Seal of the State of New Jersey is filled with meaning. The horse and the helmet near the top show the state's independence and strength. Below them, the shield with three plows on it represents New Jersey's agricultural tradition. To the left stands a woman representing Liberty, and to the right is Ceres, the Roman goddess of grain, who holds a cornucopia to show the state's bounty. Underneath them is the state's motto, "Liberty and Prosperity," along with the number 1776—the year that New Jersey named itself as a state and joined the American Revolution. (New Jersey officially became a state in 1787.)

State Flag

New Jersey's state flag dates to 1896. The state seal appears in the center of the flag. The background color is buff—a golden brown color. The dark blue color that is featured in the seal is called "Jersey blue." These two colors were assigned to the New Jersey regiments during the Revolutionary War by George Washington himself.

State Song

Every state in the country has a state song—with the exception of New Jersey. Despite repeated efforts by the state government, lawmakers have never been able to agree on a song. In the 1980s, efforts to make Bruce Springsteen's "Born to Run" the state song failed. A recent attempt to create a state song in 2014 would have recognized five different songs. This measure failed too. Red Mascara's "I'm from New Jersey" would have been the state song, while the other songs would have had different titles like "state anthem."

HISTORICAL EVENTS TIMELINE

1524

The first European explorer to reach New Jersey, Giovanni da Verrazzano, maps its coast.

1638

The Swedish found the short-lived colony of New Sweden in modern-day Delaware, Pennsylvania, and New Jersey.

1660

The Dutch found Bergen, the first permanent European settlement in present-day New Jersey.

State Tree

The northern red oak, *Quercus rubra*, is the state tree of New Jersey. It was selected by the state government because of its beauty and dignified appearance. The tree's long life and strength are also symbolic. The red oak can grow to heights of 100 feet (30 m), making it one of the tallest trees in New Jersey. In the autumn, the leaves of the tree turn a brilliant red-orange color.

State Flower

New Jersey's state flower is *Viola sororia*: the common blue violet or common meadow violet. This flower is found across New Jersey. It grows wild in nature as well as being planted in gardens. The bloom is made up of five petals that range from blue to purple in color. In 1913, the state legislature picked the violet as the official state flower, but this resolution only lasted one year. It was not until 1971 that the violet was permanently declared the state flower.

1664
The British seize control of New Jersey from the Dutch.

1776
New Jersey declares itself independent of British rule during the American Revolution.

1787
New Jersey becomes the third state.

State
Dinosaur

Hadrosaurus foulkii

2001

The September 11 terrorist attacks are responsible for the deaths of more than seven hundred New Jerseyans.

2003

The New Jersey Devils win the Stanley Cup for the third time in just nine years.

2004

The River Line opens, connecting the cities of Camden and Trenton via rail.

State Insect
Honeybee

State Animal
Horse

CURRENT EVENTS TIMELINE

2011

New Jersey receives $38 million to improve its public schools through the federal Race to the Top program.

2012

Hurricane Sandy makes landfall in New Jersey and devastates the shoreline.

2018

Democrat Phil Murphy is sworn in as New Jersey's governor.

Sandy Hook is one of forty-four oceanfront beaches in New Jersey.

1 Geography

New Jersey has a diverse landscape, from mountains in the north to coastal plains in the south. The areas bordering New York City and Philadelphia are densely populated. Much of the state is covered by farms and parks. This fact gave the state its nickname, the Garden State. This phrase was coined in an 1878 speech by Abraham Browning, a Camden man, but it was not officially recognized until 1954. That year, it was added to license plates in the state.

The Piedmont Region

New Jersey is typically divided into four geographic regions: Valley and Ridge, Highlands, Piedmont, and Coastal Plains. The Piedmont is in the northeast corner of New Jersey, where the Hudson River separates the state from New York's Westchester County and from the towering skyscrapers of New York City. This geographic region is an area of gentle hills that is about 200 feet (60 meters) above sea level. The Piedmont covers only about one-fifth of the state's land area. More than half the state's people live there, especially in the eastern part.

FAST FACT

New Jersey is the most densely populated state in the country due to its large population compared to its small size. The four most densely populated cities in the entire country, including Hoboken, are in Hudson County, New Jersey— across from New York City. Many of the state's residents live in the part of the state close to New York City.

New Jersey borders New York, Pennsylvania, and Delaware.

New Jersey's four largest cities are in the Piedmont: Newark, Jersey City, Paterson, and Elizabeth.

One of New Jersey's many pleasant natural surprises is a region of cliffs called the Palisades. Rising from 200 to 540 feet (60 to 165 m) above the Hudson River, these sheer cliffs extend north from Hoboken, New Jersey, to Nyack, New York, on the river's west bank. They were formed close to two hundred million years ago. At the time, molten lava rose from deep in Earth's crust and hardened. Today, this dramatic wall of gray-black rock with streaks of dark red adds to the beauty of the region around the Hudson River.

Another unique feature of the Piedmont is an area called the Great Swamp National Wildlife Refuge. These wetlands were created more than ten thousand years ago, during the last ice age, when the movement of glaciers carved up the land. The area, within sight of New York City's skyscrapers, was at one point chosen as the site for a new airport. But New Jersey residents protested, and in 1960, the swamp was set aside as a wildlife refuge. Today, it is home to nearly one thousand plant and animal species, including more than two hundred bird species alone. Several miles of trails and boardwalks make it a peaceful place to walk.

The decline of manufacturing industries in recent years affected some parts of the Piedmont. For example, the Hudson River waterfront became littered with rotting piers and crumbling warehouses that had been abandoned for decades. Since the late 1990s,

The Palisades are a great place to hike.

however, the state has made efforts to repair the region. Broken-down structures have been replaced by attractive apartment complexes, row houses, and modern office buildings.

The Highlands Region

A short drive to the west of New Jersey's bustling cities and nearby suburbs will take travelers to the Highlands region. This is a semi-wilderness area that covers nearly 1,000 square miles (2,600 square kilometers) of steep hills and narrow valleys. Many of the state's eight hundred lakes and ponds are located there and provide scenic recreation areas for both residents and tourists. The Highlands region is also a vital **watershed**. It supplies water to millions of New Jerseyans living to the east.

The Valley and Ridge Region

The smallest of New Jersey's land regions is located in the far northwest. The Valley and Ridge is part of the large Appalachian Mountain chain, which stretches from the Saint Lawrence River in Canada to Georgia in the south. Part of the Appalachian Trail cuts through New Jersey in this region. The trail crosses the Kittatinny Mountains, the largest mountains in the state. The state's tallest peak reaches 1,803 feet (550 m) high. Its name is fitting: High Point.

The hills in this region may not be very tall, but they are steep. This gives them a rugged appearance. The grassy valleys and hills are perfect for apple orchards and herds of dairy cattle.

The Delaware Water Gap forms the border between northwestern New Jersey and Pennsylvania. The famous Delaware Water

Buttermilk Falls are part of the Delaware Water Gap National Recreation Area.

New Jersey's Biggest Cities

(Population numbers are from the US Census Bureau's 2017 projections for incorporated cities.)

Newark

1. Newark: population 285,154

The largest city in New Jersey, Newark is a major shipping and transportation hub for the East Coast. Newark Liberty International Airport is one of three key airports that service the larger New York metropolitan area.

2. Jersey City: population 270,753

Part of the New York metro region and located across the Hudson River from New York City, Jersey City is one of the most ethnically diverse cities in the world. It also has, among US cities, one of the highest percentages of residents who work as artists.

3. Paterson: population 148,678

Formerly known as the "Silk City" due to the role it played in late nineteenth-century silk production, Paterson has been featured in works by poets William Carlos Williams and Allen Ginsberg, and in the hit TV show *The Sopranos*.

4. Elizabeth: population 130,215

Restaurants, shops, and parks abound in this lively small city, named by *Popular Science* magazine as one of "America's 50 Greenest Cities." Parts of Newark Airport are in Elizabeth, as well as the Port Newark-Elizabeth Marine Terminal.

5. Clifton: population 86,607

A small city in Passaic County, Clifton is home to colorful New Jersey landmarks such as Rutt's Hut (a deep-fried hot dog restaurant) and a number of locations where episodes of *The Sopranos* were filmed.

6. Trenton: population 84,964

Trenton is the state capital, and the state of New Jersey is the largest employer in the city. Nearly twenty thousand government employees commute into the city each workday. Trenton's famous landmarks include a monument to George Washington's 1776 victory against Hessian forces during the American Revolution.

7. Camden: population 74,532

Just across the Delaware River from Philadelphia, Camden is the location of the Campbell Soup Company headquarters and a number of medical and educational institutions. The Walt Whitman House, where the poet lived in his later years, is a National Historic Landmark in the city.

Trenton

8. Passaic: population 71,247

The neighbor of Clifton, Passaic has some architecturally interesting homes and churches. It is home to a thriving community of Orthodox Jews.

9. Union City: population 70,387

West of Hoboken, Union City has been called "Havana on the Hudson" because of its significant Cuban population. The annual Cuban Day Parade draws crowds, and the city also hosts artistic and cultural events.

Passaic

10. Bayonne 67,186

Just east of Newark, Bayonne lies on a narrow peninsula between New York Bay and Newark Bay. It is linked to New York City by the Bayonne Bridge. The city is home to the large sculpture *To the Struggle Against World Terrorism* that was donated by Russia to the United States in remembrance of the victims of the September 11 terror attacks.

Gap National Recreation Area straddles about 40 miles (65 kilometers) of the Delaware River. This is one of the most popular scenic areas in the eastern United States. It draws about three and a half million visitors each year.

The Coastal Plain Region

An invisible line runs northeast across the state, from Trenton, the state capital, to the Atlantic Coast at Perth Amboy. This is called the fall line. It is marked by waterfalls and rapids on the Raritan River and other flowing bodies of water.

The region south and east of this fall line is part of the Coastal Plain. This region begins on Cape Cod in Massachusetts and extends down the eastern seaboard to Georgia. The Coastal Plain covers about 60 percent of New Jersey's land area but holds only about one-fourth of the population.

When most people in New Jersey mention southern New Jersey, they are referring to the state's Atlantic coastline, which they call "the Shore." This part of the Coastal Plain is a long stretch of sandy beaches and barrier islands. The islands are long, narrow sandbars separated by tidal inlets (small waterways) and lagoons. Many of the islands are family-oriented resort communities. Others have nature sanctuaries. In geographic terms, the Jersey Shore is the Outer Coastal Plain. The Inner Coastal Plain is much larger and slightly elevated, though it rarely gets more than 100 feet (30 m) above sea level.

Near the fall line, the Inner Coastal Plain has suburbs and small towns, many dating back to the early 1700s. Campuses for two of the state's best-known universities—Princeton and Rutgers—are located there. The soil is excellent for farming. The northern area of the Coastal Plain has many farms that specialize in tomatoes and other vegetables, including an increasing variety of unusual vegetables from Asia.

The largest area of southern New Jersey's Coastal Plain is a 2,000-square-mile (5,200 sq km) area called the Pine Barrens, or Pinelands. The soil is not useful for ordinary farming. However, the wetland regions are ideal for cranberry bogs, and some drier areas have been turned into blueberry farms. Most of the area is under government protection as the Pinelands National Reserve. The area is home to dozens of rare plant and animal species, including plant varieties that are normally found farther south. Plants that thrive there include pitcher plants and several kinds of bladderworts. These plants are known as "meat eaters" because they trap and digest insects. The Pine Barrens also contains rare species of frogs, turtles, and snakes.

The Pine Barrens are home to fascinating plants and animals.

The beautiful Pine Barrens tree frog likes the white cedar swamps and peat moss of the Pine Barrens. This frog is regarded as a symbol of the Pinelands. It was once considered endangered, but it has done well in recent years. In 2007, the state government upgraded its status from endangered (at risk of dying out) to threatened (at risk of becoming endangered in the near future).

Cape May lies at the southern tip of New Jersey. From Cape May, the Jersey Shore extends northward along some 140 miles (225 km) of beaches and coastal islands. Fifty resort cities and towns, including Atlantic City, draw vacationers in the summer. Sandy Hook, in the north, is a 6.5-mile-long (10.5 km) peninsula that stretches into the Atlantic Ocean. Black cherry trees and ancient holly trees provide food for migrating birds. This sandy area is said to be the best place in the nation to observe migrating hawks.

The Pine Barrens tree frog is named for the Pinelands but can also be found outside of New Jersey.

Border Disagreements

New Jersey's borders are relatively simple. Most are bodies of water. The Atlantic Ocean is to the east. To the south, the Delaware Bay and Delaware River separate the state from Delaware, and to the west, the Delaware River forms the border with Pennsylvania. It is only New Jersey's northern border with New York that doesn't follow a natural landmark. Despite this simplicity, New Jersey's history is full of border disagreements with its neighbors.

King George III settled a border dispute between New York and New Jersey in the 1700s.

The surveyed line that separates New York and New Jersey led to the New York–New Jersey Line War. The dispute dated to 1664, when New York and New Jersey were originally split. The disagreement was so heated on the border that landowners came into conflict, burning each other's crops and kidnapping each other across the border. Finally, after many years of arguing, King George III settled the dispute, and both sides agreed on a compromise shortly before independence.

While this compromise fixed New Jersey's only land border, its maritime (sea) borders were still debated. The royal decree that fixed Delaware's border gave Delaware the entirety of the Delaware River. Typically, rivers are split between the states on either side when they form boundaries. American courts have upheld Delaware's rights to the entire river. In 2008, the Supreme Court even forbade New Jersey from building an industrial plant that would have stretched into the river between the two states.

New Jersey's fortunes have fared much better on the maritime border with New York. An 1834 compact between the two states split the Hudson River and the bay at its mouth. It read:

> The state of New York shall retain its present jurisdiction of and over Bedlow's [now Liberty] and Ellis's island ... The state of New Jersey shall have the exclusive right of property in and to the land under water lying west of the middle of the bay of New York, and west of the middle of that part of the Hudson river which lies between Manhattan island and New Jersey. The state of New Jersey shall have the exclusive jurisdiction of and over the wharves, docks, and improvements.

This last line was to have important effects. New York expanded Ellis Island by dumping rubble into the bay and building on it. In 1998, the Supreme Court ruled that this built up part of Ellis Island belonged to New Jersey, not New York. As a result, New Jersey was given ownership of almost 90 percent of modern-day Ellis Island.

A winter storm blankets Hoboken in snow in 2016.

Climate

New Jersey measures only 167 miles (269 km) north to south and 56 miles (90 km) wide. Despite the state's small size, its climate varies from one region to another. The coldest areas are in the northwest corner. The average January temperature there is about 28 degrees Fahrenheit (–2 degrees Celsius), and summers are cool because of the higher altitude. In the southwest, the winter temperature is about 34°F (1°C). Summers are quite warm, averaging 76°F (24°C) in July. The ocean keeps coastal temperatures warmer during winter and cooler in the summer. However, the long, low coastline is sometimes hit by hurricanes and strong winter storms called nor'easters, which sweep in off the Atlantic.

Northern New Jersey gets 40 to 50 inches (101 to 127 centimeters) of snow each year. The southernmost parts of the state get only 10 to 15 inches (25 to 38 cm). The snow can create dangerous driving conditions. However, skiing and snowboarding are favorite winter pastimes for many New Jerseyans, and the icy lakes and ponds are ideal for ice skating and hockey.

FAST FACT

New Jersey is the fifth smallest state, with a land area of just 7,354 square miles (19,047 sq km). Rhode Island, Delaware, Connecticut, and Hawaii are the only smaller states. New Jersey, however, has a variety of terrain in its small area, from mountains to coastal plains.

Environment

The varied landscapes and climate make New Jersey an ideal place for a wide range of plant and animal life. The state boasts nearly fifty state parks and forests. There are also more than one hundred special so-called wildlife management areas.

The Jersey Shore

"The Shore," as it is called in New Jersey, stretches 141 miles (227 km) along the Atlantic coast. Tourist attractions dot the coastline, and visitors from around the country and world vacation there.

At the north end is Sandy Hook—a narrow strip of land jutting toward New York City. It is part of the Gateway National Recreation Area. People come to enjoy its pristine beaches and observe the many birds that live there. It is just one place along the Shore where the state's wildlife can be enjoyed.

At the south end of the Shore is Cape May. A ferry runs from there to neighboring Delaware. Cape May is known as America's oldest seaside resort. It is a scenic town, full of historic buildings. Visitors can stroll through its streets to get a feeling for how nineteenth-century America looked.

In the middle, there are many cities on the beach, including Ocean City, Point Pleasant Beach, and Atlantic City, among many others. These cities all have their own unique atmosphere and attractions. What they share is access to amazing beaches, interesting boardwalks, and plenty to do. Miniature golf courses, aquariums, zoos, arcades, and countless restaurants dot the Shore. It's no surprise that families from all over come to spend quality time together in the sun.

Ocean City Boardwalk

Cape May is known for its historic Victorian homes, like this one.

What Lives in New Jersey?

Hammond's yellow spring beauty

Pine Barrens gentian

Flora

Hammond's Yellow Spring Beauty This rare wildflower can only be found in a small northwestern patch of New Jersey. The plant's flower is bright yellow and smaller than a dime. The Nature Conservancy is working to protect the rare flower, but its future remains uncertain.

Highbush Blueberry *Vaccinium corymbosum* is a shrub that is native to New Jersey. Its most important feature is its blueberries, which are cultivated and sold. In fact, New Jersey is the state where blueberries were first cultivated and used as a food crop. As a result, this species is now the state fruit of New Jersey.

Pine Barrens Gentian *Gentiana autumnalis* is native to East Coast pine barrens from New Jersey to South Carolina. Its beautiful flower is a brilliant blue color. Seeds typically lie under the soil and bloom when a fire burns down the forest above. Fires were once a normal part of life in the Pine Barrens. Today, however, fires are often prevented by people, and the Pine Barrens gentian is becoming rarer.

Pitch Pine *Pinus rigida* is the most common tree of the Pine Barrens and the tree that gives the landscape its unique appearance. The pitch pine is shorter than most pine trees, growing up to 60 feet (18 m) in height but often remaining shorter. It also looks more rugged than most pine trees—its branches can sprout at odd angles and its trunk can be twisted.

White Oak *Quercus alba* is found across the eastern half of the United States. It is a majestic tree that forms a wide canopy and grows up to 100 feet (30 m) in height. Until recently, the oldest white oak in the country stood in Basking Ridge, New Jersey. It was approximately six hundred years old, but it died in 2017.

Fauna

Black Bear The largest land mammal in New Jersey, black bears can be found across most of the state. They even visit urban areas, where they raid garbage cans and come into conflict with residents. Despite their size, black bears are rarely aggressive and live mostly on berries, fruit, and plants.

Brook trout

Bobcat Found mostly in northern New Jersey, bobcats are listed as an endangered species in the state. There are small populations in southern New Jersey, but people rarely spot this secretive animal. Bobcats are larger than housecats, though they rarely weigh more than 35 pounds (16 kilograms).

Brook Trout Commonly caught by fishermen, the brook trout is the state fish of New Jersey. Although it is one of four kinds of trout now found in the state, it is the only one that is native to the region. The others were introduced by people. The brook trout can grow up to 25 inches (63 cm) in length.

Eastern goldfinch

Eastern Goldfinch Also called the American goldfinch, the eastern goldfinch is known for its brilliant gold color. However, only the feathers of males during certain seasons are bright gold. Females are a duller yellow color. The eastern goldfinch is the state bird of New Jersey as well as Iowa and Washington.

Eastern Tiger Salamander The largest salamander in the state, eastern tiger salamanders are found in southern New Jersey, especially Cape May. They are born in shallow ponds and live the first part of their life underwater. As they mature, they lose their gills and move onto dry land. An eastern tiger salamander can be recognized by the irregular yellow markings on its back.

Eastern tiger salamander

Riverfront Park, Newark

These protected areas offer people a chance to view wildlife sanctuaries from roads, trails, and boardwalks, sometimes within the shadow of high-rise apartments and office buildings.

Beech, cedar, maple, poplar, birch, and oak trees are found across the state. In the fall, leaves change color, turning the landscape into a lovely blend of orange, red, and yellow. In the spring, summer, and fall, flowers bloom across all parts of the state. Flowering plants such as buttercups, azaleas, bloodroot, mountain laurels, and lilies are native to the state. New Jersey's trees, shrubs, and flowers provide both food and homes for wildlife.

Much of New Jersey's wildlife lives in the woodlands found across the state. Most of the animals common to the northeastern United States are found there. These include white-tailed deer, raccoons, opossums, red foxes, coyotes, squirrels, skunks, and rabbits. Porcupines, beavers, and bats also make New Jersey their home. Smaller numbers of black bears and bobcats continue to prowl the heavily wooded hillsides.

New Jersey is also known for its number and variety of birds. The state is on the Atlantic Flyway. This is the route that migrating birds take to their nesting grounds in Central and South America. In addition, the state's mild climate and many sanctuaries and wilderness areas create ideal conditions for nesting. Cape May might be the most famous location in the country for bird-watchers. More than one hundred thousand bird-watchers visit the area every year, and hundreds of species of birds have been seen there.

The many lakes, ponds, streams, and rivers also provide homes to New Jersey wildlife. Fish such as bass, trout, and pike swim through the waters. Lobsters, crabs, oysters, and clams live in

the state's coastal waters. Sometimes whales can be seen moving through the ocean. Ducks, geese, egrets, herons, and pelicans are among the many birds that can be seen wading and swimming in or flying above the state's waterways.

Cape May Point State Park hosts the Cape May Hawk Watch each year.

New Jersey has made protecting its rich environment a state priority. It has passed a number of laws to protect its waterways from pollution. The state is also at the forefront of moving away from fossil fuels, like oil and natural gas, toward clean energy sources, like wind and solar power. In 2018, Governor Phil Murphy began steps to make New Jersey run on 100 percent clean energy by 2050.

The Battle of Princeton took place on January 3, 1777. General George Washington led the Continental Army.

2 The History of New Jersey

ew Jersey has played an important role in American history. It was a key state during the Revolutionary War. Its agriculture fed the neighboring states of New York and Pennsylvania. And as the United States industrialized, New Jersey became a leader of industry.

The Earliest Inhabitants

Little is known about the first people who lived in present-day New Jersey. The first groups probably arrived in the region about ten thousand years ago. By the year 1600, New Jersey was home to the Lenape people. They hunted, fished, and gathered wild plant foods. They also planted crops, such as beans, squash, corn, and tobacco. They lived in small communities, sometimes built along riverbanks. Their homes, called wigwams, were made out of saplings, bark, and other plant material. The wigwams were small and usually round, though they could be long or oblong (these larger structures were called longhouses). The Lenape used materials such as animal hides,

FAST FACT
The Lenape suffered a series of disasters with the arrival of the Europeans. Colonists cheated them out of their lands. Other Native American tribes waged war against them to gain access to European trade, and outbreaks of diseases from Europe killed many. These events forced them to abandon their homeland and move west.

This image shows a typical Lenape village.

seashells, plants, and clay to make their own clothes, baskets, and pottery. Some Lenape also made swift canoes out of bark and other tree parts.

Today, the original Lenape people would hardly recognize the homeland they once called "Scheyichbi," or "the place bordering the ocean." Yet many place names in modern New Jersey come from their language. For example, the town of Absecon gets its name from a Lenape word meaning "place of swans." Manhattan (in New York) is a name derived from a Lenape word for "island of many hills." Hoboken, the name of a city in New Jersey on the Hudson River, is Lenape for "place where pipes are traded," and the Passaic River is named for the Lenape word for "river that flows through a valley."

European Colonization

The first European explorer to land on the shore of present-day New Jersey was Giovanni da Verrazzano, an Italian sea captain who sailed for France in 1524. Verrazzano, however, did not claim the land for France. Nearly a century passed before Europeans settled in this part of North America.

In 1609, Henry Hudson sailed along the New Jersey coast before entering the river that now bears his name. Hudson was an English explorer who sailed under the flag of the Netherlands. He claimed the area for the Dutch. By 1630, about two hundred Dutch fur trappers and traders had settled along the Atlantic coast. They soon had rivals in the area—Swedish colonists, who settled in present-day Wilmington, Delaware, in 1638.

The Dutch forced the Swedish colonists to surrender in 1655 and ruled the area as part of their colony of New Netherland. The colony included the town called New Amsterdam at the southern end of Manhattan Island in what is now New York City. It also included other settlements in what is now New York State. By 1660, it also included the settlement that later became Jersey City.

Soon a more powerful rival—England—claimed modern-day New Jersey and the surrounding area as its own. King Charles II of England granted the area to his brother, the Duke of York. In 1664, an English fleet sailed into the harbor of New Amsterdam and demanded the surrender of all New Netherland. The Dutch governor, Peter Stuyvesant, wanted to defend the colony, but the settlers would not support him. Stuyvesant surrendered without a fight. The English renamed the captured Dutch colony New York.

The Duke of York gave the area between the Hudson and Delaware Rivers to two friends. One of them, Sir George Carteret, had been governor of the island of Jersey in the English Channel. The new colony was named New Jersey in his honor. Carteret and his friend Lord John Berkeley attracted hundreds of colonists by offering land at very low cost. They also allowed religious freedom and gave people a voice in the government. However, the government was sometimes hostile to certain religious groups. From 1674 to 1702, New Jersey was divided into East and West Jersey, with separate capitals. In 1702, England reunited the colony. However, the two capitals remained until 1775, one at Perth Amboy, the other at Burlington.

Explorer Henry Hudson

Native Americans in New Jersey

Lenape members gather at an environmental protest in 2003.

The area of modern New Jersey was originally the home of the Lenape, which in their language meant simply "man." Early European settlers called them the Delaware Indians. The Lenape were a branch of the Algonquian family of tribes. Algonquians were among the first Native peoples to meet the European explorers who landed on the Atlantic coast during the 1500s and 1600s.

The Lenape were really a group of tribes that all spoke dialects of the same language. Young men married outside their clan, and the children they and their new wives had belonged to the mother's clan. This **matrilineal** structure was confusing to the first European explorers. In Europe, children are named for their fathers, and family names are passed down through sons.

The Lenape, whose clans included the Lenni-Lenape, the Nanticoke, and the Munsee, were expert farmers and fishermen. They developed large fishing operations and complex agriculture. To farm, they moved from settlement to settlement, depending on the season. This allowed them to plant and harvest different crops more effectively. The Lenape moved less frequently than other Native tribes farther west, and they inhabited permanent structures much of the time, rather than tepees or tents.

As European settlement increased, the Lenape were forced off their land. Expansion displaced most Native Americans in the area during the 1700s, pushing them south and west. These tribes are not extinct, but except for the descendants of New Jersey Native American people who hid or joined white society, they do not live in New Jersey anymore. Most tribes that once were native to New Jersey ended up on reservations in Oklahoma.

There are no federally recognized tribes in New Jersey. The Nanticoke Lenni-Lenape Indians of New Jersey, the Ramapough Lenape Nation, and the Powhatan Renape Indians have been recognized in the state by **statutes** and received official recognition by New Jersey in 1982. In 2012, the tribes lost their state recognition. The Nanticoke Lenni-Lenape are fighting in court to have that decision reversed.

The Lenape

Lenape tribes occupied land stretching from Delaware Bay at the south end of New Jersey to eastern Pennsylvania and southern New York.

Clans: The Lenape group of First Peoples was made up of various clans divided by language dialects, including the Lenni-Lenape, Nanticoke, and Munsee.

Homes: Lenape families and clans lived in wigwams or longhouses. Wigwams were small houses for a single family, framed with saplings and covered in mats made of bark or woven cloth. Longhouses could shelter several families at a time. This architecture was more permanent than the lean-tos and tepees of other Native traditions.

Food and Agriculture: The Lenape did not need to be as **nomadic** as other tribes because they had developed complex farming and fishing techniques. These practices could support a large population in an area. The Lenape harvested clams in southern New Jersey, farmed corn and beans, and caught large numbers of fish in the rivers of the Delaware region.

Clothing: The men wore loincloths or simple leggings, and the women made elaborate and beautiful winter cloaks. Both men and women wore fur from bears or beavers to keep warm in the winter.

Tools: Hunting was done with bows and arrows. Warriors carried heavy wooden war clubs and body-length shields of moose hide and wood.

A British Colony

Throughout the 1700s, New Jersey was a booming farming colony. Efforts to establish a whaling port in the south were unsuccessful, and business developed slowly. Some colonists thought that New Jersey was doomed to be dominated by the two large cities nearby—Philadelphia to the west and New York to the east. One New Jersey merchant said, "Our wealth ends up in those cities. We are becoming like a keg tapped at both ends."

The people of New Jersey, however, soon found that their location between the two big cities could be a source of strength. As colonial America grew and became richer, New Jersey was in a crucial position for moving goods and people between New York and Philadelphia. In the early 1700s, colonial America's first **stagecoach** service was established across New Jersey to connect the two cities. That was just the beginning. From then on, New Jersey's role as a go-between for Philadelphia and New York steadily expanded.

Fighting for Independence

From 1754 to 1763, Great Britain (which had been formed by the union of England and Scotland) fought against France for control of eastern North America. The conflict was known as the French and Indian War. Britain defeated France, but the cost of the war put the British government deeply in debt. As a result, Great Britain tried to tighten its control over trade with its thirteen American colonies and imposed new taxes on the colonies. Many colonists, known as Patriots, believed they were too heavily taxed and were not given a fair say in how they were governed.

In 1774, patriots in Greenwich in southwestern New Jersey borrowed an idea from the Boston Tea Party. They protested the British tax on tea by burning a shipload of British tea. The following year, problems between the colonies and Great Britain turned into war. Early fighting broke out at Lexington and Concord in Massachusetts. On July 4, 1776, representatives of the colonies approved the Declaration of Independence. The famous document stated that the colonies now considered themselves free from British rule. The Declaration of Independence was an important step toward making the thirteen colonies into one united, independent nation.

The fight against Britain for independence, the American Revolution, lasted from 1775 to 1783. During the war, thousands of New Jerseyans joined the colonies' Continental Army, led by General George Washington. However, other New Jerseyans, who called themselves Loyalists, wanted to stay under British rule. Some Loyalists left their homes in New Jersey to move to areas protected by the British. The governor of New Jersey, William Franklin, was among the Loyalists who left. He was the son of Benjamin Franklin, one of the leading Patriots and Founding Fathers of the new nation.

New Jersey's location made it a natural battleground. Both sides wanted control of the Hudson and Delaware Rivers. Nearly a hundred armed clashes took place in New Jersey, including three major battles: Trenton, Princeton, and Monmouth.

The Battle of Trenton is often regarded as the conflict that saved the Patriot cause in its darkest hour. In the autumn of 1776, Washington's Continental Army had been badly beaten by a powerful British force. After losing New York City and Long Island to the British, Washington

Washington crossed the Delaware River to win the Battle of Trenton.

and his battered troops retreated. They moved west through New Jersey, crossing the Delaware River into Pennsylvania. By late December, the Patriot cause seemed hopeless. Washington's once-proud army of twenty-five thousand now numbered fewer than four thousand. Many did not have winter coats or shoes.

On December 25—Christmas night—Washington led his men back across the ice-clogged Delaware River. At dawn, they surprised a regiment of German troops hired by the British and won a stunning victory in the Battle of Trenton. A few days later, Washington struck again, defeating the British at the Battle of Princeton. Those two victories gave Patriot troops much-needed confidence to keep fighting.

In June 1778, Washington's army fought the British at the Battle of Monmouth. Neither side could claim victory in the battle, but the British were forced to withdraw. The battle showed that the Continental Army could hold its own against the mighty British.

One of the most famous legends of the American Revolution grew out of the Battle of Monmouth. It is said that a heroic wife carried pitchers of water to her husband's unit. When her husband collapsed, the woman helped work one of the cannons for the rest of the battle. She was later called Molly Pitcher. In fact, her true identity is not completely certain, and some historians doubt that she even existed.

Monmouth marked the last time during the American Revolution that two major armies met in battle in New Jersey. However, the two sides

Molly Pitcher became a folk hero after the Battle of Monmouth.

fought many smaller battles over the next few years. Life remained difficult for Washington's army. The winter of 1779–1780 is said to have been the coldest of the century. At their camp in Morristown, New Jersey, Washington's men suffered severely from hunger and cold. About a hundred died from the extreme weather.

The war officially ended with the signing of the Treaty of Paris in September 1783. Great Britain recognized the independence of the newly formed United States. The last British troops left American soil a few months later.

The United States Is Born

In the summer of 1787, delegates from twelve of the thirteen former colonies—now states— met at the Constitutional Convention in Philadelphia. (Only Rhode Island did not send any representatives.) The delegates hoped to create a constitution that would provide for a strong national government while also protecting the rights of the individual states.

At the convention, New Jersey's William Paterson proposed a single-chamber legislature, or lawmaking body. In Paterson's plan, each state—even a small state such as New Jersey— would have the same number of representatives. His plan was not accepted, but it did contribute to the Great Compromise. This plan created a US Congress with two houses. States with larger populations would have more members in the House of Representatives. But in the Senate, each state would have two senators, regardless of its population.

William Paterson represented New Jersey at the Constitutional Convention.

On December 18, 1787, New Jersey ratified, or approved, the US Constitution. By doing so, it became the third state to officially join the United States. In 1790, Trenton was chosen as the new state capital.

The Great Falls of the Passaic River powered early factories in Paterson.

The Industrial Revolution

New Jersey grew and expanded with the other states of the new nation. Agriculture continued to flourish, and transportation and industry became more important. At the turn of the nineteenth century, the Industrial Revolution was changing the United States. New technologies were making industry more efficient. Alexander Hamilton, who served as the first US Secretary of the Treasury, planned a model industrial city. The city of Paterson was built at the Great Falls of the Passaic River. The water from the falls was used to create power for nearby factories. These factories used newly developed machines that produced goods quickly and at a low cost. Some of these goods included textiles, tools, and weapons.

In 1804, John Stevens from Hoboken developed a twin-propeller steamboat. In 1811, he launched the nation's first steamboat ferry service, between Hoboken and New York City. In 1825, Stevens created a "steam wagon," which ran on an iron track around his estate. This experiment helped prove that steam railroads were possible. His son Robert Stevens started one of the country's first steam railroad lines in 1831. The Camden and Amboy Railroad used a British locomotive called *John Bull*. The railroad line strengthened the economic ties between New York and Philadelphia. The famous Stevens Institute of Technology, in Hoboken, is named after the family that contributed so much to the development of the state.

The Civil War

During the 1800s, the issue of slavery divided the United States. The plantations in Southern states depended on slaves to work the fields. Northern states, including New Jersey, relied on smaller farms and on industries in which slave labor did not provide a big advantage. Many Northerners also believed that slavery was morally wrong.

In 1804, New Jersey voted for gradual emancipation (freeing) of slaves in the state. Lawmakers decided that all males born into slavery would become free at age twenty-five, and females would become free at age twenty-one. Tensions between the North and South continued to grow and led to the Civil War (1861–1865). Eleven Southern states seceded from, or left, the Union (that is, the United States) and formed the Confederate States of America.

During the Civil War, more than eighty thousand young men from New Jersey wore the dark blue uniforms of the Union army. Some people in New Jersey sided with the Confederacy, but the state as a whole remained loyal to the Union. After years of bloody battles, the Union won the war in 1865. In December of that year, the Thirteenth Amendment to the US Constitution officially ended slavery throughout the United States.

This photograph shows the officers of the Fourth New Jersey Infantry Regiment during the Civil War.

Silk workers in Paterson, 1910

Economic Growth

The economy of New Jersey continued to grow. Silk processing and other industries were developed in Paterson. Oil production became important in Bayonne, and Camden became a center for shipbuilding.

The period from the 1860s to the 1890s was known as the Age of the Robber Barons. The robber barons were powerful business leaders such as John D. Rockefeller, who made a fortune in the oil industry, and Andrew Carnegie, who did the same in the steel industry. They became very wealthy by creating **monopolies** in their fields. A monopoly is a company that controls so much of an

Andrew Carnegie

industry that it has no competition and can charge high prices for its goods or services.

New Jersey politicians saw the rise of these powerful companies as a great opportunity. The state legislature passed laws that encouraged big corporations to set up offices in New Jersey. Monopolies were illegal in other states, but New Jersey allowed them. By the late 1800s, roughly half the nation's largest corporations had established headquarters in New Jersey.

The Twentieth Century

The American people became upset with the spread of monopolies. In the early 1900s, President Theodore Roosevelt and other reformers worked to break up these powerful companies. In New Jersey, the reform leader was Woodrow Wilson. He served first as president of Princeton University and then as governor of New Jersey. Wilson was elected president of the United States in 1912 and 1916. In 1917, he led the nation into World War I.

New Jersey played an important role during World War I and World War II, which the United States entered in 1941. Hundreds of thousands of troops trained and gathered at Camp Dix (later Fort Dix) and other facilities in the state before heading off to war. The state's industries produced wartime products, including chemicals, weapons, ships, and aircraft engines. New Jersey also became a leader in military research and technology.

The most notorious media event of all time occurred between the World Wars. On October 30, 1938, actor-director Orson Welles broadcast a radio drama that sounded like a real news broadcast. *The War of the Worlds* described a landing by Martians on a farm near the New Jersey town of Grover's Mill. Thousands of

Soldiers at Camp Dix prepare to fight in World War I.

listeners missed the on-air warnings that the invasion was not real, and some panicked.

The size of the panic is in dispute. There were reports of thousands of New Jersey residents jamming highways in an attempt to flee from the Martians. Some people now believe these reports were exaggerated by newspapers, which were upset that radio stations were taking away some of their advertising. They printed stories about a wide panic to make it look like radio newscasts could not be trusted. The *New York Daily News* published a large headline that read: "Fake Radio 'War' Stirs Terror Through US."

After World War II, many white people from Newark, Trenton, and other New Jersey cities began to move to surrounding areas, called suburbs. This shift was fueled by a boom in auto sales. To keep up with the growing number of vehicles on the road, New Jersey built two major roadways in the 1950s. Completed in 1951, the New Jersey **Turnpike** quickly became one of the busiest highways in the country. The Garden State Parkway connected the busy northern suburbs with resort areas along the Atlantic Coast.

As suburbs prospered, many cities in New Jersey began to crumble. Many African Americans either could not afford to move to other areas or were not allowed to move because of discrimination. Some manufacturing plants moved out of the cities as well, taking away jobs and tax revenue. City governments could not maintain important services. Living conditions in cities got worse, and tension between blacks and whites increased. Riots broke out in Newark and other cities in the late 1960s.

After an economic slump in the mid-1990s, the urban areas of New Jersey began to recover. Along the Hudson River, decaying wharfs and empty warehouses were replaced by modern

The *New York Daily News'* coverage of *The War of the Worlds*

FAST FACT

Industry has played an important part in New Jersey's history, and the state is often on the cutting edge of technology. In 1961, at a General Motors plant in Ewing Township, New Jersey, a human worker was replaced by a robot. It was the first time in history this had happened, but it would not be the last.

Important People in New Jersey's History

Buzz Aldrin

Born and raised in Montclair, New Jersey, Buzz Aldrin later graduated from the US Military Academy at West Point. After flying combat mission in the Korean War, he became an astronaut. On July 20, 1969, he became the second man to walk on the moon during the *Apollo 11* lunar landing mission.

Dorothea Dix

Dorothea Dix worked around the country to improve care for the mentally ill. During the Civil War, she became the superintendent of female nurses. Afterwards, she lobbied to have a new psychiatric hospital built in New Jersey. Near the end of her life, she stayed in a private suite in that hospital until her death in 1887.

Thomas Edison

The famed inventor Thomas Edison did most of his work in New Jersey. It was there that he invented the motion picture camera and the incandescent lightbulb. Today, the Thomas Edison Center at Menlo Park honors the inventor and educates visitors about his achievements. The city of Edison, New Jersey, was also named in his honor in 1954.

Toni Morrison

The acclaimed author Toni Morrison grew up in Ohio. In 1989, she began teaching at Princeton University in New Jersey. Four years later, she received the Nobel Prize in Literature. She was the first African American woman to receive the prestigious award. Her most famous works include *Song of Solomon* and *Beloved*. Princeton University named a hall in her honor in 2017.

Buzz Aldrin

Toni Morrison

Alice Paul

This native of Moorestown, New Jersey, was a leader of the women's suffrage movement—the campaign to secure the right to vote for women. She led protests for years, demanding equal rights for women. In 1920, her efforts paid off with the passage of the Nineteenth Amendment. It forbids states and the federal government from stopping women from voting.

Alice Paul

Paul Robeson

Born in Princeton, New Jersey, Paul Robeson attended Rutgers University and earned his law degree from Columbia University while playing professional football. However, opportunities to practice law were limited for African Americans at the time. He became famous for acting and singing in the 1920s. Later in life, his career suffered when he spoke out against racism and inequality.

Paul Robeson

Walt Whitman

The famed poet Walt Whitman was born on Long Island. His collection of poems *Leaves of Grass* is considered an American classic. It was first published in 1855, but Whitman continued to revise it and release different editions for more than forty years. Whitman spent the last nineteen years of his life in Camden, New Jersey, where his house still stands as a historic landmark.

Woodrow Wilson

A Southerner by birth, Woodrow Wilson moved to New Jersey when he began teaching at Princeton University. He later became the university's president and launched his political career when he was voted governor of the state in 1910. Popular reforms he passed in New Jersey propelled him onto the national stage. He was elected president in 1912, and he led the country through World War I.

townhouses, apartment buildings, offices, and shopping malls. Rotting piers and junk heaps gave way to parks, small-boat harbors, and recreation areas. Dozens of New York City companies moved to these renewed areas.

The Twenty-First Century

New Jerseyans have fought over reducing the bad effects of industrialization and development and have worked to protect the environment. In 2007, the state passed a law requiring a 20 percent cut in greenhouses gas emissions by the year 2020. Greenhouse gases such as carbon dioxide contribute to global warming—the slow rise in worldwide temperatures. However, in 2011, Governor Chris Christie pulled the state out of the Regional Greenhouse Gas Initiative, a nine-state program designed to reduce greenhouse gas emissions. At that time, New Jersey's greenhouse gas emissions were already below the 2020 requirements. In 2018, Phil Murphy became governor and introduced his own clean energy initiative.

Another impact on the environment in New Jersey was Hurricane Sandy, which devastated the New Jersey coastline in 2012, destroying homes, flooding businesses, and damaging key tourist attractions and boardwalks. New Jersey has since rebuilt many of the attractions, and the tourist industry is on its way back to full health. Surprisingly, the hurricane damage may lead to economic growth—billions of dollars had to be spent on new roads, new buildings, and new infrastructure, which meant that thousands of new jobs were created.

Hurricane Sandy caused nearly $30 billion of damage in New Jersey.

A Budget Crisis

In 2017, the federal government passed a tax reform bill. One small aspect of the reform was

The Miss America Competition

The history of the Miss America pageant is tightly linked to Atlantic City. It began there in 1921 and has been held there for most of its history. The 2006 to 2013 pageants were held elsewhere, but since then it has once again taken place in Atlantic City. States crown their own winners each year, and these winners from each state face off in New Jersey.

The pageant is made up of different events, such as showcasing a talent. Until recently, one event was a swimsuit competition. Women were judged by their appearance. In its early history, wearing revealing swimwear was banned in Atlantic City. The pageant had to receive special permission to allow it for the event. In 2018, however, the pageant announced that the swimsuit competition was over. Women would no longer be judged by their physical appearance. The event was rebranded the Miss America *competition*, rather than pageant.

Going forward, the competition will focus on issues like community service and conversations with judges. The winner is still expected to be a spokesperson for issues that matter and to be someone who can relate to young people. Crowned Miss America winners travel the country, speaking to crowds and changing the world for the better.

Miss America contestants pose together in Atlantic City in 2016.

to end a tax break for people who paid state income tax. This change hit residents of New Jersey, and other high-tax states, especially hard. Unfortunately, New Jersey was already struggling with its own budget issues. For the past thirty years, New Jersey has been operating with a budget deficit. A deficit occurs when spending is greater than the money raised. Because of the deficit, New Jersey has been borrowing more and more money.

Today, there is a budget crisis because of this long history of budget deficits. Tax money the state takes in is still far less than the money it spends each year. State pensions also contribute to the problem. Employees like teachers and government workers were promised pensions—money paid out to them after retirement. However, the state government did not set aside enough money to guarantee these pension payments. During budget crises, the pensions were often underfunded. Without even greater government spending on pensions, the state will not be able to pay retired teachers and government workers.

Protesters march in Trenton in 2014 to demand that Governor Christie fund their pensions.

The situation is quite serious. A 2017 report by the group Truth in Accounting ranked the finances of every state. It ranked New Jersey as the worst in the country and estimated its debt at $209 billion. That means the state owes $67,200 for each of its taxpayers. Currently, the state cannot reduce this debt since it is still running a budget deficit.

How exactly to navigate the budget crisis is one of the greatest issues the state faces today. It is likely that spending or pensions will have to be cut. But there is strong political pressure against this. Taxes in the state are already high, and federal tax reform increased this burden on state residents. A solution to this problem will require compromise by Republicans and Democrats.

Today, industry is run on electrical power. But early in New Jersey's history, it was water power that ran mills. Waterwheels harnessed the power of flowing water to grind wheat into flour, spin cloth, and roll metal into sheets.

Make Your Own Waterwheel

Cooper Gristmill in Chester is open to visitors.

Supplies

- Two Styrofoam or stiff paper plates
- Small disposable plastic or paper cups
- Masking tape
- A pencil

Directions

1. Push the pencil through the center of the plates.
2. Place a cup on top of the outside edges of the two plates (between them). The side of the cup should be resting on the plates. Tape the cup into position.
3. Turn the plates just far enough to fit another cup next to the first one on top. Make sure the opening of the cup is facing the same way as the previous cup's opening.
4. Tape the next cup into place and repeat the process until the two plates are covered in cups on all sides. The cups need to be lined up so that the opening of one cup is next to the bottom of the next cup all the way around.
5. Make sure the plates are loose enough to spin freely on the pencil. Holding both ends of the pencil, put your waterwheel under flowing water like the faucet and watch it spin. Try holding it in different directions under the water to see which way works best.

Atlantic City is home to more than 30,000 New Jerseyans and hosted 24.1 million visitors in 2017.

3 Who Lives in New Jersey?

ew Jersey is home to a vibrant population. The state ranks as one of the most diverse in the nation, with thriving communities from around the world. In 2017, Wallethub.com found Jersey City to be the most diverse city in the entire country. The US Census found that more than forty languages were spoken there. New Jersey's diversity is one of its great strengths, and it's a source of pride for its residents.

Early Immigration

Over the past few centuries, New Jersey's population has undergone changes similar to those in other parts of the Northeast. More than three-quarters of the colonists in New Jersey in the 1700s could trace their origins to Great Britain and Ireland. The same was true of the people in New York and the New England colonies. Many Dutch and Swedish settlers and their descendants also made New Jersey their home.

After 1800, shiploads of immigrants from Europe arrived at New Jersey ports and other ports throughout the Northeast. In the 1840s, the number of immigrants increased dramatically,

FAST FACT
Immigrants who were born in another country make up 22 percent of New Jersey's population. This places it in the top-five states for percentage of foreign-born residents. Immigrants in New Jersey tend to be better educated than people born in the state, and they contribute billions of tax dollars each year in state and local taxes.

Immigrants from Europe arrive at Ellis Island in 1907.

especially from Ireland and Germany. In Ireland, a blight, or disease, struck the potato crop. Potatoes were the major source of food and income for many people. The countryside was devastated, and more than a million people lost their lives. Others escaped the famine on ships bound for the United States. During the same period, large numbers of German immigrants fled from the political problems in their homeland to start new lives in the United States.

Many of the new immigrants headed for New Jersey cities, hoping to find factory jobs. They often met anger from native-born Americans. Some people disliked the newcomers' unfamiliar customs and were afraid that immigrants would take jobs away from them. Over time, the newcomers overcame the prejudice and fear. Many young Irish women found jobs as household servants. Some German families opened restaurants, butcher shops, and "beer gardens." Other immigrants worked in factories, hospitals, and stores. Many became firefighters or police officers or joined the clergy. Some pursued higher education. Despite limited opportunities, the immigrants became lawyers, doctors, writers, and teachers. Some eventually became active in politics.

The 1880s started a new period of immigration. More people were coming to the United States than ever before. Many arrived from other parts of Europe, such as Russia and what is now Poland. Large numbers of immigrants from Italy settled in New Jersey. The state's population continued to increase through the 1900s.

A Diverse Population

Since the early 1970s, New Jersey's population has become even more diverse. Changes in the nation's immigration laws led to an increase in new arrivals from regions other than Europe. In recent decades, people from Spanish-speaking countries in Latin America and people from Asian countries have come to New Jersey in larger numbers than before.

The Cuban Day Parade in Union City celebrates Cuban heritage.

The Little India neighborhood in Jersey City

New Jersey's population is constantly changing. Between 2010 and 2013, the Hispanic and Asian populations each increased by at least 5 percent. Two out of five Asians in New Jersey have roots in India. Indians are the fastest-growing immigrant group in the state. The next-largest groups of Asian immigrants are people from China, the Philippines, and Korea.

Also, the number of "Baby Boomers" (those people born during the years following World War II) who are between the ages of sixty and sixty-nine increased by more than 6.5 percent as people aged and moved to the state and the birth rate fell. New Jersey is becoming more ethnically diverse, and older.

Hispanics are the largest minority group in New Jersey. They make up about one-fifth of the state's population, and their numbers are growing. Half of the Hispanics in the state are under the age of thirty.

The influence of many different immigrant cultures can be seen across New Jersey. Large communities of people from the same ethnic group can be found in cities across the state. Restaurants and other businesses that sell food and goods from abroad are very popular. A walk down a main street in Hoboken or neighboring Jersey City can reveal a worldwide sampling of shops and restaurants—Brazilian, Cuban, South African, Chinese, Greek, and Sicilian. Additionally, many cultural events and festivals celebrating the heritage of different ethnic groups are held throughout the state.

FAST FACT

India is the country where the largest number of New Jersey immigrants were born. Indian Americans, however, are a diverse population in themselves. They may speak Hindi, Gujarati, or English at home, depending on their background. They also follow many different religions. About half of Indian Americans are Hindu. Others are Christian, Muslim, or Sikh.

The African American Community

In the 1800s, African Americans made up only a small portion of New Jersey's population. As slavery in the state came to an end, free African Americans worked at different types of jobs. A few owned farms, and a larger number worked as farm laborers. Even after the Civil War ended, life was often hard for them. Jobs were scarce, and prejudice was widespread.

This painting by Jacob Lawrence shows African Americans moving north during World War I.

The United States fought in World Wars I and II in the first half of the twentieth century. New Jersey's factories and shipyards had to quickly manufacture the weapons and equipment needed by America's military forces. Thousands of African Americans moved north from Southern states to find work. Many African Americans found jobs as laborers. Over the years, others found work as scholars, doctors, lawyers, teachers, business owners, and much more.

For twenty years after the end of World War II in 1945, many people moved to growing New Jersey suburbs, leaving the crowded cities behind. Few African American families could afford such a move, and white people and real estate agencies in suburbs would often not rent or sell homes to African Americans. Most cities and suburbs were segregated, meaning that black families could find housing only in black neighborhoods.

The frustrations of African Americans increased during the civil rights movement of the 1950s and 1960s. Dr. Martin Luther King Jr. led protest marches through the South. He and other civil rights leaders helped force Southern cities and states to remove laws that discriminated against African Americans.

Racial tensions existed in Northern states too. In the late 1960s, race riots broke out in Northern

FAST FACT

While New Jersey remains the most densely populated state in the country, its growth has slowed recently. In 2017, the state's population grew just 0.3 percent. The national average was 0.71 percent. This slow growth may have a negative effect on the state's economy and lead to higher taxes if it is not stopped.

cities. One of the worst riots occurred in Newark in July 1967. Twenty-six people were killed, and more than one thousand were wounded. Rioters caused more than $10 million in property damage.

Like other Northern states, New Jersey launched programs to try to modernize cities and create more opportunities for African Americans. More low-income housing was built. New state colleges had lower tuition fees, making them more affordable to New Jerseyans from all walks of life. A commuter railroad improved transportation, and job training programs were established.

Today, African Americans make up about one-seventh of the state's population and are very active in the politics, education, and businesses of the state.

New Jersey's Appeal

Why do people live in New Jersey? That is a question with many answers. Some residents enjoy the quiet, country life offered by farmland in the south. The shoreline is popular with people who enjoy the ocean and beaches. Many people are drawn to New Jersey by its schools. Some New Jersey schools are among the highest-rated in the nation. In the 2018 *US News* Best High School rankings, twenty-three New Jersey schools earned gold medals, including High Technology High School in Lincroft. It was ranked number twenty-two in the country. New Jersey is also home to fine universities and colleges that attract students from across the country and around the world.

Other people move to the state because of the job opportunities it offers. Large corporations have been based in New Jersey for a long time. Recently, more corporate offices and research companies have moved out of New York City to New Jersey to take advantage of greater space,

Blueberries, the state fruit of New Jersey, can be used to make all kinds of delicious desserts. If you have the right pan, blueberry muffins are an easy-to-make treat.

Blueberry Muffins

Supplies and Ingredients

- A muffin (or cupcake) pan
- Muffin cups that fit your pan
- 1½ cups all-purpose flour
- ¾ cup sugar
- 2 teaspoons baking powder (not baking soda!)
- ½ teaspoon salt
- ⅓ cup canola or vegetable oil
- ⅓ cup milk
- 2 small eggs or 1 large egg
- 1 cup washed fresh blueberries

Directions

1. Begin by preheating your oven to 400 degrees Fahrenheit (200 degrees Celsius).
2. Mix the flour, sugar, baking powder, and salt together in a large mixing bowl.
3. In a separate bowl, beat an egg (breaking the yolk and blending it into the egg white). Then, add the oil and milk to the egg and mix.
4. At this point, you have a bowl of dry ingredients and a bowl of liquid ingredients. Add one to other and mix them with a fork until they have combined. Don't stir them too much, just enough for the batter to have no clumps.
5. Add the blueberries and fold them in.
6. After putting muffin cups in your pan, fill the cups up halfway with the batter. It will rise as it cooks.
7. Put the muffins in the preheated oven for fifteen minutes. Take the pan out and test them by sticking one muffin with a toothpick or fork. It should come out dry, not covered with batter. If there is batter, put the muffins back in for five more minutes.
8. After you let them cool, enjoy your blueberry muffins!

New Jersey's Celebrities

Jon Bon Jovi

Jon Bon Jovi was born as John Francis Bongiovi Jr. in Perth Amboy. In 1984, his rock band, Bon Jovi, released their first album. It was a smash hit. Jon Bon Jovi and his band continue to tour the world and release new albums. In 2018, the band was inducted into the Rock and Roll Hall of Fame.

Derek Jeter

Born in Pequannock, Derek Jeter was an incredibly gifted baseball player from a young age. He was selected as High School Player of the Year in 1992 and drafted by the Yankees after graduation. He played shortstop for the Yankees for nearly two decades and was a five-time World Series champion.

Gaten Matarazzo

Kevin Jonas

Kevin Jonas was the only member of the Jonas Brothers born in New Jersey. (All of the brothers grew up in Wyckoff, though.) The Jonas Brothers became famous in 2007 when they released a self-titled album. Kevin Jonas also appeared in a reality TV show, *Married to Jonas*, about him and his wife living in New Jersey.

Gaten Matarazzo

Born in Little Egg Harbor Township, Gaten Matarazzo started his acting career on Broadway. In 2016, he got his big break, starring as Dustin in the Netflix show *Stranger Things*. This role catapulted him to Hollywood stardom.

Cristin Milioti

Cristin Milioti

A native of Cherry Hill, Cristin Milioti grew up in New Jersey. She went on to build a career on Broadway and in Hollywood as an actress. She won a Grammy for Best Musical Theater Album for her work in the play *Once*. On television, she starred in the sitcom *How I Met Your Mother*.

Shaquille O'Neal

Basketball legend Shaquille O'Neal was born in Newark. The 7'1" (2.2 m) center is one of the most famous players in National Basketball Association (NBA) history. He won four NBA championship games and played for six different teams over his long career.

Zoe Saldana

Originally from Passaic, Zoe Saldana first performed as a ballerina. She later appeared on television and in movies. In 2009, she starred in the blockbuster film *Avatar*. Saldana has also appeared in *Star Trek* and *Guardians of the Galaxy* films, among others.

Shaquille O'Neal

Bruce Springsteen

New Jersey's most celebrated son is likely Bruce Springsteen. Born in Long Branch, the singer-songwriter focused on his working-class New Jersey background in the lyrics of many of his hits. Over the course of his career, he has won twenty Grammy Awards and sold more than sixty-five million albums. Through it all, he never forgot his roots in New Jersey, and the state has always celebrated its association with "The Boss."

Zoe Saldana

Martha Stewart

Martha Stewart was born in Jersey City in 1941. As a teen, she worked as a model. After attending college, Stewart started a successful catering company. She used her experiences as a caterer to write books about entertaining. Stewart's books were the stepping stone to international fame. Today, her lifestyle brand includes magazines, television shows, home goods, and more.

Bruce Springsteen

An NJ Transit light rail trolley picks up passengers at Washington Station.

lower rents, and lower taxes. These businesses create jobs in factories, offices, and stores.

New Jersey's location is attractive to commuters. Many New Jerseyans live in suburbs outside cities where they work. People call these suburbs "bedroom communities"—places where city workers sleep. Several bridges and tunnels cross the Hudson River to New York City, and bridges span the Delaware River to Philadelphia. Commuters can travel by train, bus, or car, and some can conveniently cross the Hudson River by ferry. Highways may be crowded, and trips may be long, but for many commuters, living in New Jersey is worth the trouble.

In the past, New Jersey's population was spreading out into suburbs from urban centers. But for the first time since the 1940s, this trend is now reversing. Cities near New York City are seeing a wave of new arrivals, while suburbs on the outskirts of cities are shrinking. If this trend continues, it will be a big shift in where people choose to live in New Jersey.

New Jersey's Biggest Colleges and Universities

1. Rutgers University–New Brunswick, Piscataway

(35,641 undergraduate students)

2. Montclair State University

(16,852 undergraduate students)

3. Rowan University, Glassboro

(15,401 undergraduate students)

4. Thomas Edison State University, Trenton

(15,238 undergraduate students)

5. Kean University, Union

(11,984 undergraduate students)

6. William Paterson University of New Jersey, Wayne

(8,838 undergraduate students)

7. Rutgers University–Newark

(8,551 undergraduate students)

8. New Jersey Institute of Technology, Newark

(8,483 undergraduate students)

9. Stockton University, Galloway

(8,275 undergraduate students)

10. Fairleigh Dickinson University, Teaneck

(8,214 undergraduate students)

All enrollment numbers are from *US News and World Report* 2019 rankings.

Rutgers University

Montclair State University

Rowan University

Thomas Edison State University

A History of Immigration

New Jersey has always been a popular state for immigrants. In part, this is due to its location near Ellis Island—the port where many immigrants arrived between the late nineteenth and early twentieth centuries. From New Jersey's earliest history to the present day, many new Americans have chosen to settle in the Garden State. Their hard work and pride in their new home help make the state great.

In the early twentieth century, immigration resulted in rapid growth in New Jersey. Between 1900 and 1930, the population of New Jersey doubled. This growth was much faster than other states at the time. Large numbers of immigrants from Europe, especially from Germany and Ireland, were behind the rapid growth. In 1900, New Jersey was the sixteenth most populous state in the country. But just ten years later, in 1910, it was the eleventh. That same year, more than one-quarter of New Jerseyans had been born outside of the United States. The percentage of foreign-born residents then was even higher than it is now. They helped make New Jersey a center of industry in the country.

A Portuguese neighborhood in Newark shows off the state's exciting diversity.

By the 1960s and 1970s, the percentage of foreign-born New Jerseyans had dropped to less than 10 percent. Briefly, the state was largely made up of people born in the United States. But that began to change when the United States changed its immigrations laws in 1965. The changes made it easier for people from outside of Europe to come to the United States. New Jersey once again attracted large numbers of immigrants. The new immigrants were mostly from Latin America and Asia, rather than from Europe as in the past. Over time, the percentage of foreign-born residents rose from less than 10 percent to the current rate of 22 percent.

The immigrants of today are incredibly diverse. According to 2016 census estimates, the largest number come from India. Indian Americans, however, make up just 12.6 percent of foreign-born New Jerseyans. The remaining 87.4 percent come from other countries. After India, the Dominican Republic, Mexico, the Philippines, China, Colombia, and Ecuador are the most common countries of origin.

Most immigrants can speak English fluently. Nevertheless, communities around New Jersey often celebrate and keep using their native languages. In neighborhoods around the state, you can find signs in dozens of different languages. Ethnic restaurants are common across the state. They provide immigrants with a taste of home and give all Americans a chance to try something new.

Newark is home to factories of all kinds.

4 At Work in New Jersey

New Jersey's economy is quite diverse. Farms, factories, research centers, and businesses that cater to tourists cover the state. The economy is also helped by New Jersey's position on the East Coast, close to New York City, Philadelphia, and Washington, DC. New Jersey is within a day's drive of 40 percent of the United States' population. This is a huge benefit to companies looking to distribute goods to many Americans or be close to workers in other major American cities.

Agriculture

Much of New Jersey is covered with cities and suburbs, and large areas are protected wetlands or wildlife preserves. Yet close to 20 percent of the land area is still devoted to farmland.

There are over nine thousand farms in the state. Most are fairly small and family owned. Prosperous dairy farms and orchards cover the hillsides of the northwestern corner of the state. In the northeastern corner of New Jersey, greenhouses and nurseries produce many types of colorful flowers. Many flowers grown there end up in New York City markets. On the level

FAST FACT

New Jersey's workforce is highly educated. More than one in three residents have at least a bachelor's degree. By this measure, it is the fifth most educated state in the country. This is a great benefit to the state's economy. Companies that need highly educated workers can expect to find them in the Garden State.

lands just north of the Pine Barrens, farms produce a variety of vegetables, especially tomatoes, sweet corn, lettuce, and beans. New Jersey's Pine Barrens is home to some of the country's largest cranberry bogs. New Jersey is also one of the top blueberry-growing states.

A New Jersey cranberry bog at harvest time

Although fishing is not a major New Jersey industry, the long coast is an excellent source of clams. The coastal waters are also good for catching flounder, lobsters, and oysters.

Science, Technology, and Health Care

Albert Einstein conducted research at the Institute for Advanced Study.

New Jersey is known as the state where the famed inventor Thomas Alva Edison had his laboratories. The state is also the home of the Institute for Advanced Study in Princeton, where the scientific genius Albert Einstein did research from the mid-1930s to the mid-1950s.

Another well-known research organization with facilities in New Jersey is Bell Laboratories. Many drug companies, computer companies, and aerospace research firms are also based in the state. The large **pharmaceutical** and health care products company Johnson & Johnson has its headquarters in New Brunswick, as well as research centers and offices elsewhere in the state.

New Jersey's closeness to New York City gives its businesses a boost.

The health-care industry is also one of the most important industries of New Jersey's economy. About 12 percent of workers in the state work in health care, from doctors and nurses to office personnel.

Industry

New Jersey has a long industrial history. The state has been a leader in industrial development since the mid-1800s. Smoke once hung over the cities as machines churned out an incredible variety of products in large quantities—shoes, machine parts, chemicals, furniture, and dozens of other items. During both World Wars, New Jersey turned its industrial might to the production of weapons and ammunition. The state has been losing manufacturing jobs in recent years, but some areas are growing. Manufacturing jobs in the state often require special skills, and they usually pay well.

Today, New Jersey is a national leader in making drugs and other medical products, its biggest manufacturing industry. The related field of **biotechnology** has become a key industry too. Biotechnology is the use of biological materials and processes to make useful products, such as pharmaceuticals.

Another big area is the production of chemicals, including such household products as cleansers, soaps, and shampoos. Computer and electronic products have grown in importance. New Jersey is also one of the top states in food processing, including freezing and canning foods and producing wholesale baked goods.

Shipping

The Port of New York and New Jersey is the largest port on the East Coast. Major port facilities, operated by the

Goods are shipped globally from Bayonne.

Hackensack University Medical Center

Port Authority of New York and New Jersey, are located in Newark, Elizabeth, and Jersey City, as well as in New York City. In 2016, more than $187 billion worth of cargo entered or left the United States through the Port of New York and New Jersey. The port provides jobs for thousands of New Jersey workers.

A Changing Economy

Like that of other states, New Jersey's economy has become increasingly geared toward service industries. About three of every five New Jersey workers have jobs in this sector. Service industries include transportation, education, health care, banking, and insurance. People who work in retail stores, restaurants, and hotels are also part of the service industry.

Tourism

Throughout the state's history, people have visited New Jersey to enjoy all it has to offer. Today, tourist activities bring in close to $40 billion in revenue each year, and tourism provides jobs for one in ten New Jersey workers.

In 1934, during the Great Depression, Charles Darrow, an out-of-work salesman, sold a game he called Monopoly to the Parker Brothers game company. The properties on the board were all named after real streets in Atlantic City. Although many people say Darrow did not invent the game himself, he helped make it one of the most successful board games in history. Today, at the real corner of Boardwalk and Park Place, a brass plaque honors Darrow for his achievement.

Tourism got a big boost after casino gambling became legal in Atlantic City in 1978. The city's hotels and famous boardwalk had made it a popular vacation spot for a hundred years, but it had been in decline in recent decades. Once gambling was permitted, developers and investors moved in to create glittering resorts that rivaled those in Las Vegas. By 2014, competition from new casinos in neighboring states hurt business in Atlantic City, leading to the closing of four of its eleven casinos.

Atlantic City draws tourists from all over.

People visit New Jersey's cities to attend plays, movies, and concerts. The state's museums are widely respected. The state has a battleship museum, an agricultural museum, and many history museums and historical sites. Of course, the Garden State also has many beautiful public gardens.

The Liberty Science Center in Jersey City features exhibits and hands-on activities, as well as educational programs for students. The center is located in Liberty State Park, on the western shore of Upper New York Bay. Ferries from Liberty State Park take visitors to the Statue of Liberty and to Ellis Island.

Sports fans have plenty to cheer about in New Jersey. The New Jersey Devils, the state's pro hockey team, play at the Prudential Center in Newark. The Jets and the Giants football teams may represent New York, but they play their home games at the $1.6-billion MetLife Stadium at the Meadowlands constructed in

Fans cheer on the New Jersey Devils at the Stanley Cup playoffs in 2018.

Pinelands National Reserve was the first national reserve in the United States.

2010. The Meadowlands is also home to one of three major horse racing tracks in the state. The New York Red Bulls, a Major League Soccer team, are also based in New Jersey. They play at the Red Bull Arena in Harrison.

Protecting the Environment

Throughout most of the 1900s, New Jersey's factories produced a wealth of products, but they also created gloomy clouds of smog. Rivers and lakes were polluted with chemicals and waste.

In the last part of the century, the state made progress in cleaning up rivers and streams. Abandoned factories and shipyards were replaced with modern housing and recreation areas. Special attention was also paid to the state's native plants and animals. State lawmakers introduced strict rules regarding pollution and land development.

Private organizations such as the Nature Conservancy and the New Jersey Audubon Society have helped promote policies that save open spaces. In 1978, for example, the Pinelands National Reserve was established to limit development and protect the environment. The reserve covers 1,700 square miles (4,400 sq km) of the Coastal Plain. This large area was the country's first national reserve. Much of it is forested land that can be reached only by foot.

One bold plan involved the development and protection of the Hackensack Meadows, commonly known as the Meadowlands. This region of marshlands and ponds was created by the last ice age. Different agencies manage the land and try to protect native plants and animals and control pollution. The land has also been used to develop a unique area that

Manufacturing has undergone major changes in the United States. As it became cheaper to produce goods in other countries, American manufacturing declined. In recent years, the industry has bounced back. High-tech, specialized manufacturing has grown.

In New Jersey, clean energy has powered a manufacturing revival. Companies that specialize in solar and wind energy have taken root in the state. They were drawn in part by state government programs. Energy efficiency has also driven growth in manufacturing. Efficient heating and air conditioning units as well as special lightbulbs and windows reduce energy costs for households. These products are made in factories in New Jersey and installed by workers in the state.

As of 2017, more than forty thousand New Jerseyans were employed by clean energy companies. These jobs are often high-paying and require a specialized and highly educated workforce. Growth in the sector is driven by small businesses rather than large corporations.

Further government programs are being considered to grow this industry even more in the future. But whether or not they pass, the industry is here to stay. It is spurring increased manufacturing in the state and bringing in wealth and jobs. It is just one way that the state's economy is responding to changes in the twenty-first century.

Creating Clean Energy

Wind turbines harness the power of the wind to provide clean energy.

Solar panels in Piscataway protect parked cars while generating power.

Feeding a Nation

From its early history, New Jersey has been an important source of food for the United States. Usually, people think of agriculture—farming and raising animals—when they think of the food industry. While New Jersey is no longer a leading state in agriculture, it is a leader in other parts of the food industry, like manufacturing, research, and distribution.

Campbell Soup Company was founded in New Jersey and is still based there today. It was in New Jersey that condensed soup was first invented and exported. Removing some of the water from soup made it much more efficient to distribute. New Jersey remains a leader in food innovation. Scientists work to make food cheaper and healthier in the Garden State.

Another company based in New Jersey is Goya Foods, the largest Hispanic food producer. The food and agricultural industries employ more than 440,000 people in New Jersey! These companies are drawn in part by New Jersey's location as well as its workforce. Food can be delivered by truck from New Jersey to much of the East Coast. The massive Port of New York and New Jersey allows food to be imported and exported from the country too.

Goya Foods' headquarters is in Jersey City.

includes major sports and entertainment facilities. The Meadowlands area is an example of how New Jersey's residents and agencies can work together to protect the land while also finding ways to help the economy.

Economic Slowdown

At the end of 2007, the United States entered a recession. A recession is when the economy shrinks rather than growing like usual. The so-called Great Recession officially ended in June of 2009. But its effects lasted longer. Many people struggled to find work, and wages did not rise.

New Jersey was especially hard hit by the recession, although every state suffered. Before the economic downturn, New Jersey's unemployment rate—the percentage of people who cannot find work—was just 4 percent. In January of 2010, it reached 9.8 percent. However, in July of 2018, New Jersey finally saw its unemployment rate drop to 4.2 percent. After nearly a decade, New Jersey had mostly recovered.

The future of jobs in New Jersey looks bright. At the beginning of 2018, Governor Phil Murphy assembled a panel of experts to look at how New Jersey can further improve its economy. Murphy also campaigned on raising the minimum wage—the least a business can pay a worker—from $8.60 to $15 an hour. This would nearly double the income of workers earning the minimum wage. It remains to be seen if this proposal will become law.

The New Jersey State House is one of the oldest state capitols in America.

5 Government

The state capital of New Jersey is Trenton. It is there that representatives from across the state gather to govern and make laws. Lawmakers as well as the governor meet and have their offices in the New Jersey State House. The decisions they come to there have far-reaching consequences for residents of New Jersey. From funding schools to building roads, the state government affects the daily life of citizens in many ways.

Government Structure

Every state has different layers of government. From the smallest village to the largest city, nearly every community has a government. There are more than five hundred of these communities—or municipalities—in New Jersey. These include cities, towns, townships, boroughs, and villages. Most cities are governed by a mayor and a city council. There are many other local bodies with important powers, such as school boards, planning boards, zoning boards, and water commissions.

Cities, towns, and townships are grouped together to form counties. New Jersey has twenty-one counties. They are governed by

FAST FACT
Blue states tend to vote for Democrats, while red states tend to vote for Republicans. Today, New Jersey is considered one of the bluest states in the country, but this was not always the case. Before 1992, New Jersey was often won by Republican presidential candidates. Between 1992 and 2016, Democratic candidates for president carried the state in every election.

Trenton City Hall

groups called boards of chosen freeholders. This term dates back to colonial times, when only men who owned property, called freeholders, could vote or hold office. The counties handle a wide variety of responsibilities, involving schools, roads, hospitals, and other key areas.

The next level is state government. The governor, the governor's staff, the legislature, and the judicial system work together to create and uphold laws and run the government. New Jersey has a large degree of "home rule," which means that under the state's constitution and laws, local governments have more power than they do in many other states.

As of 2018, New Jersey had fourteen representatives in the US Congress in Washington, DC. Voters in New Jersey elected twelve members to the US House of Representatives. Like voters in all other states, they also elect two US senators.

Branches of Government

The Executive Branch

Governor Phil Murphy took office in 2018.

For a long time, New Jersey was one of the few states that had no lieutenant governor. The lieutenant governor is like the vice president of the state. In 2001 and again in 2004, the governor of New Jersey resigned and was replaced by the person who was president of the senate. Then, in November 2005, New Jersey voters approved an amendment to the constitution that created the position of lieutenant governor. Since 2009, the lieutenant governor has run for office on the same ticket as the governor. The lieutenant governor takes over if the governor resigns or dies in office. The governor and lieutenant governor are elected to four-year terms. Other officials such as the attorney general, secretary of state, and treasurer, are appointed by the governor.

The Legislative Branch

The legislature is made up of two houses: the senate and the general assembly. The senate has forty members, and the general assembly has eighty. Members of the assembly are elected every two years. Senators serve four-year terms, except the first term of a new decade, which is only two years.

The Judicial Branch

The court system has several divisions. Municipal courts hear cases for minor offenses, such as traffic tickets and shoplifting. Municipal judges are appointed by the local government. Each county has a superior court, which hears cases involving criminal, civil, and family law. People who do not agree with the outcome of their case can have it reviewed by an appellate court. New Jersey also has a tax court. The supreme court is the highest court in the state and hears the most important cases. Judges for the superior, tax, and supreme courts are selected by the governor and must be approved by the state senate. Judges on these courts serve for a seven-year term. After that, they can be chosen to stay on the court until they reach the age of seventy, at which time they must retire.

The New Jersey supreme court has seven justices, or judges.

Creating a New Law

Ideas for new state laws often come from concerned citizens, but any proposed law, called a bill, must be officially submitted by an assembly member or a senator. A committee studies the bill and may **amend**, or change, it. Committees have public meetings where people from the community may speak about the bill. If the committee approves it, the bill is then debated in the house in which it was first proposed.

New Jersey lawmakers vote on a bill in 2011.

Legislators may argue about the bill and amend it further. A bill passes if it receives a majority of the vote—twenty-one votes if it is in the senate, or forty-one if it is in the general assembly. If enough members of one house vote for the bill, it is sent to the other house, where it goes through a similar process. If the second house approves the bill, it goes on to the governor. The governor can approve the bill or may decide to **veto**, or reject, it. If the governor does not take any action on the bill, it can become a law. If the governor vetoes the bill, it can still become law if two-thirds of both the senate and the general assembly vote for it.

Both legislative houses can also propose amendments to the state constitution. If three-fifths of the assembly and the senate approve the amendment, it goes on the ballot in the next general election. The amendment passes if the majority of voters approve it. The current state constitution has been amended more than thirty times.

Politics

New Jersey's strong emphasis on home rule has encouraged many citizens to make their views known to local and state officials. Citizens may also run for many types of local office. Many of these positions are unpaid, but they offer the person a role in making decisions that affect the community. However, some people say that New Jersey has too many local bodies that have too much power. Over the years, New Jersey officials have sometimes abused these powers. Some were convicted of accepting bribes in return for granting contracts or giving favorable treatment to certain businesses.

New Jersey has a majority of Democratic Party voters who usually elect a majority

Keeping Up with Politics on Social Media

In a democracy, it is important to stay up to date with politics. If you do not know what is going on in your community, you will not know whom to vote for. In the past, this meant reading the newspaper and talking to neighbors. Today, social media can help people keep up with current issues.

Twitter is one platform that political parties and politicians use to express their ideas. The Republican Party in New Jersey uses @NJGOP, while the Democratic Party uses @NJDSC. Both parties tweet about their important political battles. They also retweet statements from important politicians in the state. Often, both parties will tweet very different views on the same issue.

When using Twitter and social media, it is important to remember that sometimes information can be biased. Political parties and politicians tweet things to support their cause. They might ignore good arguments the other side makes on purpose. Occasionally, tweets even contain incorrect information. It is a good idea to hear both sides of an issue for this reason. Comparing the claims of both sides of an argument helps you pick out false or misleading statements. If you are aware of these problems, social media can be a valuable tool for staying involved in politics. Of course, always ask a trusted adult before going online.

The Twitter accounts for the New Jersey Democratic Party and the New Jersey Republican Party provide up-to-date information about politics.

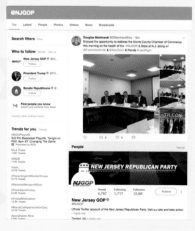

Democratic senate and house. The governor's mansion, however, frequently changes hands. In 2010, Chris Christie, a Republican, took over as governor. He delivered the keynote speech at the Republican National Convention in 2012. Christie was a rising star of the Republican Party.

Christie easily won his 2013 reelection campaign for governor with 60 percent of the vote. His strong leadership in the aftermath of Hurricane Sandy had made him quite popular in New Jersey. However, his second term as governor was marked by a serious political scandal: Bridgegate.

The Democratic mayor of Fort Lee had opposed Christie's reelection as governor. As a result, two of Christie's aides conspired to close the important George Washington Bridge from Fort Lee to New York City one morning. This act of political revenge caused a massive traffic jam. There was no proof that Christie ordered the closure of the bridge, but the scandal hurt his reputation. His popularity in New Jersey plummeted.

At the end of Christie's two terms, Democrat Phil Murphy and Christie's lieutenant governor, Kim Guadagno, faced off in the 2017 election for governor. Phil Murphy won handily with 56 percent of the vote. Guadagno received only 42 percent. As is often the case in New Jersey, the governor's mansion changed hands between the two major parties.

Glossary

amend To change, often related to a constitution or legal document.

biotechnology The use of biological materials and processes to make useful products, such as medicines.

matrilineal The family line based on motherhood.

monopoly A company that controls so much of an industry that it has no competition and can charge high prices.

nomadic A way of life characterized by moving frequently from place to place.

pharmaceutical Related to the production and development of medicines or drugs.

stagecoach An enclosed horse-drawn carriage, often used to carry people and mail.

statute A law.

turnpike A highway on which a toll is charged at intervals.

veto The president's and governor's right to reject a proposed law.

watershed An area of land whose rivers and streams all flow into the same body of water.

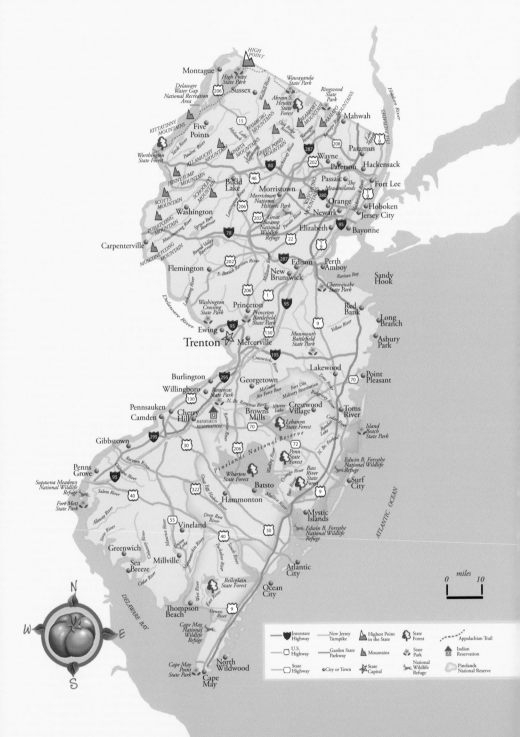

HIGH POINT

Montague

High Point
State Park

Delaware
Water Gap
National Recreation
Area

Sussex

Wawayanda
State Park

206

Abram S.
Hewitt
State
Forest

Ringwood
State
Park

KITTATINNY MOUNTAINS

HAMBURG
MOUNTAINS

15

Five
Points

RAMAPO MOUNTAINS

Mahwah

Worthington
State Forest

SPARTA
MOUNTAINS

ALLAMUCHY
MOUNTAINS

GREEN POINT
MOUNTAIN

287

Wayne

208

Paramus

202

JENNY JUMP
MOUNTAIN

SCHOOLEYS
MOUNTAIN

Budd
Lake

80

46

Paterson

Passaic

Hackensack

THE PALISADES

Hudson River

SCOTTS
MOUNTAIN

POHATCONG
MOUNTAIN

Washington

206

Morristown

Morristown
National
Historic Park

Great
Swamp
National
Wildlife
Refuge

WATCHUNG
MOUNTAIN

280

The
Meadowlands

Fort Lee

Orange

Newark

Hoboken

Jersey City

Carpenterville

MUSCONETCONG
MOUNTAIN

78

202

Round Valley
Reservoir

22

Elizabeth

95

Bayonne

Flemington

202

S. Br. Raritan River

287

Edison

New
Brunswick

Perth
Amboy

9

Raritan Bay

Sandy
Hook

Washington
Crossing
State Park

Princeton

206

Princeton
Battlefield
State Park

1

95

Cheesequake
State Park

Red
Bank

Long
Branch

Ewing

95

130

Monmouth
Battlefield
State Park

9

Yellow River

Asbury
Park

Trenton

Mercerville

195

Crosswicks River

Lakewood

Point
Pleasant

Burlington

295

Georgetown

McGuire
Air Force Base

Fort Dix
Military Reservation

70

Toms River

Willingboro

130

Rancocas
State Park

N. Br. Rancocas River

Mirror
Lake

Crestwood
Village

Ridgeway River

Pennsauken

Camden

Cherry
Hill

RANCOCAS
RESERVATION

Browns
Mills

70

Lebanon
State Forest

Cedar River

Toms
River

Island
Beach
State Park

Gibbstown

295

30

Pinelands National Reserve

206

72

Penn
State
Forest

Batsto River

Bass
River
State
Forest

Edwin B. Forsythe
National Wildlife
Refuge

Surf
City

Penns
Grove

95

Raccoon River

Great Egg Harbor River

Wharton
State Forest

Mullica River

9

Supawna Meadows
National Wildlife
Refuge

Salem River

40

322

Batsto

Fort Mott
State Park

Alloway River

Deep Run
River

Hammonton

Stow Creek

55

Vineland

Manumuskin River

30

Greenwich

Maurice River

Union River

40

Mystic
Islands

Edwin B. Forsythe
National Wildlife
Refuge

ATLANTIC OCEAN

Sea
Breeze

Millville

Cedar River

Tuckahoe River

Atlantic
City

Belleplain
State Forest

Ocean
City

DELAWARE BAY

Thompson
Beach

Wilt River

East River

Dennis River

9

Cape May
National
Wildlife
Refuge

North
Wildwood

Cape May
Point
State Park

Cape
May

N
W E
S

miles
0   10

Interstate
Highway

New Jersey
Turnpike

Highest Point
in the State

State
Forest

Appalachian Trail

U.S.
Highway

Garden State
Parkway

Mountains

State
Park

Indian
Reservation

State
Highway

City or Town

State
Capital

National
Wildlife
Refuge

Pinelands
National Reserve

New Jersey State Map and Map Skills

Map Skills

1. What is the northernmost state park in New Jersey?

2. What river forms New Jersey's western border?

3. What interstate runs alongside the southern half of the New Jersey Turnpike?

4. Through which ridge of mountains does the Delaware Water Gap National Recreation Area cut?

5. What town or city is closest to Monmouth Battlefield State Park on this map?

6. What river is Millville located on?

7. What US highway goes through Trenton?

8. Are there more mountains north or south of Newark?

9. What is the southernmost city or town in New Jersey?

10. What bay is west of Sandy Hook?

More Information

Books

Misztal, Maggie. *The Colony of New Jersey*. New York: PowerKids Press, 2015.

Stewart, Mark. *The New Jersey Devils*. Chicago: Norwood House Press, 2014.

Yomtov, Nelson. *New Jersey*. My United States. New York: Scholastic, 2017.

Websites

The Nanticoke Lenni-Lenape Tribal Nation—About Us
http://nanticoke-lenapetribalnation.org/about
The official website of the Nanticoke Lenni-Lenape Tribal Nation
provides information about the modern tribal government
and a link to their online museum at the top of the page.

New Jersey: The Garden State
https://kids.nationalgeographic.com/explore/states/new-jersey
National Geographic Kids profiles New Jersey and
presents interesting facts about the state.

Visit New Jersey—Thing to Do
https://www.visitnj.org/things-to-do
New Jersey's official tourism website provides a
list of things to do in the Garden State.

Index